Praise for *Water & Wave*

With the uncanny clarity of the born observer, Eugene Datta, standing at the site of a martyr's death in Ganderbal, Kashmir, recalls how "An old woman / sobbed without tears as oblong drops / of the mustard field shone through holes in her earlobes." Or he is in a coffee shop in Jadavpur, West Bengal, recalling his student days there, "and the lost faces wrapped / in that damp smell of the south wind in spring / (which made the heart twinge, / without fail, / in that one special way / that couldn't be named)." What becomes clear, as Datta moves fluidly across boundaries of countries and cultures, and his own past and present, is that he is an extraordinary writer—cosmopolitan, erudite, achingly lyrical. His poems remind me of why I came to poetry in the first place.

— George Bilgere

From delicate haiku-like miniatures in which "thoughts lie white / on the black filigree / of branches," to "January 2022," a poem wide-ranging enough to encompass simultaneous global disasters, Eugene Datta knows that to imagine pain "isn't equal to suffering it." Even so, the poet's ability to comprehend—that is, to both understand and hold close all that he observes—is lovingly confirmed in poems whose agile language serves a deeper purpose: to acknowledge, with empathy, the shadows and light of worlds both seen and unseen. Throughout *Water & Wave*, Datta's vision is distinguished by a meditative openness that wisely asks, "if you can receive as a mirror / does, without effort, without bias, / everything in front of it, / ...who can tell / if you haven't, for that instant, for all / your flaws, been a bodhisattva?" In the light of such poems, Eugene Datta's benevolent intelligence shines.

— Ned Balbo

Water & Wave

POEMS

EUGENE DATTA

REDHAWK
PUBLICATIONS

Redhawk Publications
The Catawba Valley Community College Press
2550 US Hwy 70 SE
Hickory NC 28602

ISBN: 978-1-959346-51-7

Printed in the United States of America

Layout by Katherine Hickman

Cover design by Melanie Zimmermann

Cover photograph by Eugene Datta

Author photograph by Anastasia Datta

redhawkpublications.com

For Natalia, Anastasia, and Yannick

Thus everything depends on something else.
And that on which it depends is never independent.

Santideva

What do we do to those we need,
To those whose need of us endures
Even the knowledge of what we are?

Philip Levine

Contents

Water & Wave

SITTING ON A PARK BENCH ON A SNOWY EVENING

The thoughts lie white
on the black filigree
of branches.

Where my head should be,
the sound of snow-
flakes.

THOUGHTS

Though they'd vowed
not to leave, though I had

chained them to the bed
closest to my pillow,

the room was empty
when I rose in the morning.

UNUSED

Between a red house
and an unkempt hedge, a white
chair in unmown yard—
the flakes of its peeling paint
open like petals in spring.

THE PLACE FROM WHERE

A tall tree with lush boughs in front of me.
Next to it, a smaller tree with bare branches.

A red brick house behind the trees. On either side,
more trees and houses, parts of them hidden.

Hedges, garden sheds and slices of garden.
Bare branches etched against the clouds, and birds

flitting from perch to perch. Looking at them, I look
for the place from where they're being seen this way,

the place where they're being known as seen, and find
only the trees, the houses, the hedges, the garden sheds,

the slices of garden, the bare branches etched on the clouds,
and the birds flitting from perch to perch.

EQUILIBRIUM

A tangle of leafless branches
and twigs across a wire fence,

and through it the winter sky:
patches of blue, gray and white,

twilight-washed, reflected
in the pond where bathing, ice

skating or feeding the ducks
are forbidden. In a little yawn

of cloud-less water, the twin
contrails of an airplane are a taut

arrow, which turns, with a sudden
gust of wind, into the droopy slither

of a snake on its way to the next
sky-dune, from where,

as the water stills, flocks of birds
fly.

MONSOON

Daybreak. The rain has stopped:
the betel palm leaves are a bouquet
of green tongues,
dripping.

The garden path is full of young snails,
hundreds of them, crawling
in all directions, past hundreds
of crushed ones, some still dying.

THE CLOSER TO THE WATER THE BETTER

We were strolling
      through a neighborhood we didn't
          know, and found

a small pond lit up
      by street light, the water
          churning with fish.

We leaned on the fence
      for a closer look
          and talked about how nice

it must be to live in one
      of the houses facing the pond—
          the closer to the water

the better, we decided.
      Then we heard some-
          thing fall into the pond,

followed by a horse laugh—
      we saw two teenage boys
          on the other side

and a cat thrashing in the water.
      By the time we reached
          the spot, the boys had

fled and the pond had turned
      still. Behind us,
          in the house closest

to the water, its windows
      brightly lit, it was
          the quiet of a nice evening.

CYCLONE

From the airplane the coastline looked
       like a watercolor gone wrong,

daubs of blue in places that should have
       been green. It was ominous

even to the inexperienced eye,
       but the real horror lurked below,

among the coconut palms standing
       like stunned armies of pole-shaped

Kanishkas, heads stolen by the invader.
       Death was in full bloom,

bloated carcasses waiting in vain
       for the vultures taken by the storm.

The wind took my friend away
       in front of my eyes, a man said—

they'd looked for shelter under
       the cantilever of an office building.

Bodies too full of water lay half-burned,
       piled high in a ghastly pyramid.

A boy and his sister, orphans now, stood
       holding each other's hands—where

their home had been, a few neighbors,
       pools of water, and a dead cow.

SPRING

Young graves marked
with green and white headstones,
the earth around them grassless.

The narcissi are in full bloom
in the cemetery: paperwhite
petals and blue-green leaves.

Spring is cold in Kashmir.

GANDERBAL

In a field of mustard, the house was a jagged sea
        of collapsed roof, walls, door-frames, windows—

burnt wood, shards of glass, mangled sheets of tin—
        and rocks and bricks, some stained with blood.

Out of a tall stand of poplars beyond the field,
        the widow came, three small boys in tow, barefoot

in the cold, and stood staring at what had been
        their home, the youngest clutching the hem

of his mother's disheveled phiran. An old woman
        sobbed without tears as oblong drops

of the mustard field shone through holes in her earlobes.
        There were other children, faces

streaked with fear, and a narrow canal
        lined with bare trees. Veiled faces gazed

out of windows back in the martyr's village; his father
        hit his own head against a brick wall, again

and again, as the women wailed and others
        stared in silence. Thin spirals of smoke rose

to the spring clouds hanging low over Ganderbal.
        My son got what he wanted, the father said.

ANJAR, 2001

The pyres go on burning like constellations from across lightyears.
The years, more than twenty of them now, haven't doused
those flames.

In the makeshift tent, under layers of borrowed relief blankets,
sleep played a reckless hide-and-seek with demented gusts
of wind.

What did the young man say when we asked him about the body
they were carting away? The midday sun scorched what was left
of the place.

How can you cremate this person without knowing if they
were Hindu? we'd asked. The shape of a human foot
in the flattened flesh.

We don't know, he said. No one is alive to tell who was who.
We cremate the bodies we retrieve, the Muslims bury the ones
they find.

An odd balm to the fractured air gasping to the noise of hammers
and drills, and excavators removing debris. We stood on a roof
a meter or so high.

A cry had oozed faintly from beneath slabs of concrete until
almost an hour ago. Only mangled toys in its place now; festoons
of dusty, warped things.

Attar-scented fingers of a stoic stranger, pir-like, touched
the handkerchiefs covering our faces. His family lay buried some-
where, or was cremated.

In a hotel room with cracked walls our last night stayed
in the custody of a contraband bottle. We left
with a life's worth of nightmares.

The orchid that almost died
is bowing under the weight
of new flowers

IT WOULDN'T BE ALMS

We didn't have either the time or the willingness,
but couldn't refuse the ride when he took off his phiran

and in one swift, unbroken move, in the blink of an eye,
folded the long wool garment into a neat cushion for two

and placed it on his rough-and-ready sled of raw, damp wood.
Guilt-ridden, we let him pull us along Gulmarg's lonely

snow-covered promenade, so that it wouldn't be alms
that he'd take from us, but payment for his labor. They'd had

no visitors there for days, thanks to the war, and he hadn't had any
work. But he wouldn't touch, he said to us, money he didn't earn.

A GOOD NAME

Do you remember that first flood
in Canning? she asked,

a bag of bones wrapped in what was left
of a mud-white sari. It took my son,

cows and home. Her clotted-
smoke eyes squinting against the heat

of the summer noon. I cannot see
well, and my girl—she, too, is old now—

is stone-blind. The other son brought us
to the city and died soon after—stones

in the stomach, they said. Dust-
caked feet shook in ancient Hawaiian

slippers with mismatched straps. Give me
what you can, baba.

The ding of a single one-rupee coin
dropped in the empty bowl

made a smile rise like a crescent
moon. My name, she said,

is Sumati (*she who has good intent*)—
it's a good name. Give it to a daughter

if you have one, or a niece, or some child
you love as your own.

THE SPOT

He was a friend's namesake

and sat with his back against the wall of St. Michael's/
St. Dimitrios Church on Jesuitenstraße—

at the same spot on the sidewalk
for the six or so years that I'd known him,
in good weather and bad.

We spoke every time I stopped

to drop a coin or two in his Starbucks coffee cup—
sometimes just a *hello* and a *thank-you*,

a *you're-welcome* and a *have-a-good-day/weekend.*
Sometimes he'd ask about my children—*All well?
Enjoying school? Looking forward to (*or *Enjoyed) the holidays?*

He spoke to many others—

the church he had his back to reflected on the glass façade
across the yard in front of him—

blond hair, blue eyes, and gentle
like the one whose namesake he was. It's good to give
to both charity and individuals, he'd said to me once.

The charities do a lot but sometimes we have other needs.

His need at the time was to raise enough money
for a driver's license, so that he could look for a job—

you couldn't get one without that, he said. *No, I don't need
any clothes, thank you!*—head tilted to a side, eyes
squinting, one more tightly against the light than the other.

28

Why was he on the street? *Long story*, he said.

Someone who looked like he could be the custodian
of the once-Jesuit and now-Greek (Catholic-somewhen-

in-between) church wore black clothes and a black docker hat—
he sat close by on the steps of the church, or stood there,
watching sunlight and shadow strike endless poses in front of him,

leaning into each other like tango dancers.

I'd never seen the two men speak,
but they must have known each other well.

The seasons changed, and with them the angle of light
that filled the open yard, which filled with and emptied of
school children every weekday—

the daily ebb and flow of life my friend's namesake witnessed

from his more-or-less fixed point of view.
His hair grew long and thin, his face wrinkled and shrank.

He looked like he'd given up on the driver's license.
Often, walking past him, I'd catch a whiff of weed in the air.
One day, he wasn't in his place on the sidewalk

and approached me from another side of the street—

could I spare something? I couldn't—I didn't have my wallet
on me; no change in my pocket, either.

He'd never *asked* for money before and never since,
always letting his paper cup do the job for him. That I couldn't
offer anything that day hadn't changed the way he smiled.

Then Covid came.

Familiar faces disappeared behind the strangeness of masks
if they didn't disappear altogether.

Gesund bleiben, he said to me often. You, too, I'd tell him.
He sat there wearing a surgical mask,
maintaining his distance.

The pandemic was nearing its end—there was hope

of life soon returning to normal. In that climate of relief
it occurred to me one day

that the spot on the sidewalk had been empty for weeks.
Then I found someone else sitting there. Dropping a coin
in his cup, I asked if he knew the one who sat there before.

He's dead, the man said.

I didn't ask his name.
I saw him several times. We exchanged greetings.

Take good care of yourself, I'd tell him. Yes, of course, he'd say.
You too! After some time, he didn't sit there anymore.
I never saw him again.

And I never found out what had happened to *him*.

Since then I've seen at least two men occupying that place—
I haven't asked either of them any question.

I don't know if the man in the black docker hat
really was the church custodian—I haven't seen him in months,
although on good days, sunlight and shadow still dance

their slow noontime tango at the same spot.

A TALL HOUSE WHERE THE POND WAS

After it had rained for days, and the nights had
had enough of the horny frogs, and the crows

cawing like a million faulty alarm clocks, the sun
was out again. On the roof of the old house

across the pond, a woman stood drying her hair:
every few minutes, she bent her body back, first

to the left then to the right, flicking her hair
up in the air with the back of her palms, first the left

then the right, her arms' nimble whips
quick as lightning. Clothes dried on a line strung

between posts at two ends of the roof. Every few minutes,
a wave, cloud-like, swelling up as if to lure the rain.

The next day was the last day of August in 1990.
Things have changed since then: a tall house stands

where the pond was; a tall house where I was.
Who knows where that cloud-hair is coaxing rain.

THE WALL

One morning in March, the wall came down—the whole
length of it at the same time, twenty moss-covered feet
or so. It fell on its own, suddenly, with a deep, dull
thud, burying the neighborhood's early-morning lull.

They talked about how it was a miracle that no one
was hurt; how the wall had chosen to fall just when
there was not a soul, not even a dog or a cat,
on the lane along its length. It was a mystery, they said.

A little like the disappearance of the man who'd built
the wall, to protect his small piece of land with its vegetable
garden—one day, years ago, his neighbors got to know
that he'd gone missing. Just like that. There was no

plausible reason to explain his sudden disappearance.
No one ever saw the man again. For some time,
his wife believed that he would return. His daughter,
on the other hand, never talked about her father.

The narrow, tar-coated gate that hung on the wall got used
to the fixed angles of light, the memory of movement
erased from its hinges. No one ever opened the gate again.
An ambush of weeds wiped out the vegetable garden.

Then it was left to the cats, sitting face to face on the wall,
to spell spring. The years passed in sequences of mundanity
and forgetting, and the wall, carrying the same graffiti, stood,
obedient to an absence, as long as it possibly could.

AMBER

At the Indian Coffee House
        in Jadavpur, I counted cigarette burns

on tabletops that might once have
        been a certain shade of blue Formica.

Sunlight shredded the un-swept floor hourly
        at different angles,

voices and laughter swirled with dust
        and smoke, the street below clogged

with honking rickshaws, motorbikes,
        cars, and taxis. I don't remember

the books I read sitting there, the full-
        year diaries filled with notes,

the conversations, the scent of the hands I held
        erased from the memory of scents.

I don't miss the greasy onion pakoras
        they served there with watery ketchup,

and the black filter coffee ("infusion"
        to the regulars) to wash them down—

the waiters in their tunics from another time,
        remote like comic-strip

maharajas, and the greedy, brazen crows
        on the window ledge—

but give me what's left of all this,
        and the lost faces, wrapped

in that damp smell of the south wind in spring
       (which made the heart twinge,

without fail, in that one special way
       that couldn't be named), so I can

tuck them away for safekeeping,
       each in its own state of decay

like a million-year-old insect inclusion
       in fossilized amber. So that, someday,

holding one like a gem in the sunlight,
       I can meet a moment, see a face,

hear forgotten words, their sudden music
       pouring out of the translucence like clear rain.

LONELY PLANET

A night train rattled through a valley where no one lived—
       like a zipper slider, it tightened the wrap of darkness
in its wake.

On the sidewalk of a city street, a boy woke early, the night
       lingering in his eyes: a tree quilt-stitched
to the night

by pulsing dots of light. The boy's mother folded a quilt,
       family-sized, dirt-colored, riddled with holes
like stars in the sky.

His father, raw-boned, sat dreaming; behind him a sign read
       The City of Joy—no telling if they could read the sign;
if they knew

what it meant. The tree shuddered to the engine's whistle.
       The first of the buses and taxis rattled by—
a single crow pecked

at a plastic bag of trash as the boy yawned. The train rumbled
       closer, undoing the tree—a volley of stars
rose to the reachable sky.

TRAVEL NOTES

in memory of Abhijit Gupta

In Phuentsholing, a man stood outside
        a paned window in the middle of the night,

his body a pitch-black cutout against the moon-
        light. He poked his head through a missing

pane, a hand, thrust through another hole
        in the window, trying to untuck the mosquito

net. You lay still, holding your breath, watching
        and waiting for the next scene to unfold.

Sound of angry voices and breaking glass
        in the next room. Young travelers with little cash,

you'd looked for a cheap place and found one.
        The pencil drawing has yellowed with age—

a hastily made portrait of a small boy sitting
        on a boulder as his mother washed clothes

in the Thimpu Chhu—no date, no signature, no
        name of subject or place, poor as you were

at record keeping. Friends made on the way
        treated you to Old Monk and Chop Suey

in Hotel Bhutan. You couldn't yet imagine
        such an event could lead to anything as permanent

as life-long bonds. With no money for the last
        night's rent, you imposed yourselves on people

you barely knew—they fed you, letting you
        sleep in their house, and you let their kindness

keep you warm as you waited for the sun to rise.
        Outside, the ground was covered with frost.

THEN IT RAINS

A pianist on stage:
        his body bent
like a bow,
        the audience still.

In the darkness
        behind closed eyes,
threads of sound flit
        like rain.

Somewhere, the sound
        of drums & horns
rises above the sea
        wind and the howl

of pines, herons & gulls
        flying against
storm clouds:
        it's a funeral march—

the doms make merry
        when a loved one
dies and cry
        when a child's born.

A storm rages
        as they sing
to their drums & horns.
        The pianist

takes a bow.
        Then it rains.

HIBISCUS

In a room with two curtained windows and two doors, two men sat face to face in wicker chairs. One in his early eighties, almost half a century older than the other. There are facts of life, the older one said, that we simply cannot grasp. Our intelligence is pitifully limited, no matter how hard we pretend it isn't. The younger man nodded. We're too full of ourselves, too blind with ego to see the acts of God. Maybe, the young man thought, but *God?* He kept quiet. The drone of a ceiling fan overhead. The old man mentioned Ramakrishna, the 19th century Bengali sage believed to have seen goddess Kali with his own eyes. The young man noticed a shine in the old man's eyes. Somebody once asked Ramakrishna, can your Kali make a blue hibiscus bloom next to a red one? Ramakrishna said yes with absolute certainty, the old man said. And the next morning, strolling in his garden, the thakur found a blue flower next to a red one. *On the same branch of the same tree.* Can your *science* explain this? the old man asked, his chin jutting out. Maybe, maybe not, the young man thought, but said nothing. The fan's whir filled the silence. The curtains danced. The red flowers printed on them might have been hibiscus.

Sunlight on a red floor
a pair of feet, an ant stops
a damp stain, shining

THE FOOT FROM BHUJ, A PHOTOGRAPH

No one knew whose foot
it was, there was no one left
to help the photographer find the name
of the body it belonged to.

Showing through chunks
of concrete that hid the rest
of the body, the foot, the right
one, with blood-red toenails,

anklet limp against the skin,
toe ring glinting, traveled far, in folds
of newspaper, dazzling eyes
and hurting hearts wherever it went.

DOCUMENTARY

A girl's face—a Tutsi? a Hutu?—

& a single drum beating—
in the church where she hid—

scared of the Hutus/Tutsis—
for days and nights.

Heaps and heaps of corpses—
Tutsis/Hutus—

where her eyes once were.

NOT OUR COLORS, BUT OUR COLORS NOW

Snow, late this season, finally arrived
in Aachen the day Russian tanks rolled into Ukraine

and fear kept joy company. It rained the next day
as bands of blue and yellow fluttered

outside the city hall—not our colors,
but our colors now. Four days later, on Rose Monday,

the carnival called off, I sat on a park bench
as my son and his friend, both seven, ran

after each other, pushed their scooters uphill, climbed
trees and swapped Pokémon cards.

An Indian father, out for a walk with his half-
Ukrainian daughter, aged eight, said they worried

about their family in Ukraine. ~~I didn't~~
I couldn't tell them my children were half-

Russian. A hundred-odd meters away
college students threw and kicked a small rugby ball

in bright sunlight, wearing blue and yellow.
The married life of Yaryna and Sviatoslav is as old

as the war—we hope it survives
the carnage as we watch lives turn to ashes—stilled bodies

of children covered with debris, cardboard scraps
and blood-soaked blankets—we hope, as rage keeps

despair company, as we re-think who we are and wear
blue and yellow—not our colors, but our colors now.

LEAVING IRPIN

after a photograph by Jérôme Sessini
—*The New Yorker, March 12, 2022*

He was going away; he was leaving
Irpin—his suitcase still upright, waiting—

a trustful dog next to the master's body:
the hand that held it, half-open, blood-

smeared, the right foot pointing away.
Who's the one lying close by? A friend?

A brother? A co-escapee? Half-covered, half
on the sidewalk, across curbstones painted

yellow and white, plastic waste strewn
around. What's on the mind of the soldier

kneeling on the monument? Head bowed
in grief, flag in hand, flowers in front of him,

two bodies behind—it's much harder, he's
learned the hard way, to do good than bad;

so many more ways for things to go wrong
than right. Three men with bags in hands

leaving now—lucky to be late, to be in time,
lucky to be leaving. A willow weeping

behind a shattered roof, a slate-gray sky
crisscrossed by overhead lines—

a farewell exhaled in haste covering the body,
the suitcase still upright, waiting—

JANUARY, 2022

A volcano has erupted in the Galapagos Islands,
          a twisting lace of orange
searing the landscape: no harm yet to the people
          or the pink land iguanas.

A mushroom cloud rises from the Pacific Ocean,
          grooves of gray, sepia and white
billowing from swirls of teal. After the tsunami
          Tonga braces for the pandemic.

On the coronavirus world map the colors deepen—
          from yellow to orange to red
to purple—with rising numbers of new cases,
          though fewer people are dying from Omicron.

If you're lucky to have been unharmed, you ~~do not~~
          cannot know what it's like to be
otherwise. There's no such thing as objective
          experience. You cannot fathom

the absolute value of anything, let alone life
          and death. Imagining pain isn't
equal to suffering it, and knowing there's suffering
          changes nothing.

BETWEEN STARTING POINT & DESTINATION

in memory of S.V.

If you know the end, which in this case
          you do, you'll arrange the preceding details

depending on how you remember and grieve—
          a hot, moonless night in June, a small car

racing down a narrow highway some-
          where in north India, music playing on

the car stereo, a man and a woman—not
          related but together in what's granted

by time suspended between starting point and
          destination, the abandon of the no-

man's-land between point *a* and point *b*—
          they're headed for the hills. Depending on

how you imagine and hurt, you'll see the driver's
          free hand kneading the woman's thigh—

denim-clad, or under a cotton skirt, perhaps
          with mirror work, the type she liked—like

an ocean grinding a thirsty shore, and
          the woman yielding sweetly, like asphalt

under car tire, her breath quickened, gaze,
          unseeing, fixed on the on-rushing night,

her hair whipping the air, and the air blasting
          her mind clean of trepidation and guilt,

her flesh melting under his grip, shivers
       racing to all nerve-ends. You'll imagine

milestones, trees, road-side buildings, other
       cars racing past, none of which the lovers

can see, drunk as they are on the warm air
       slapping their faces, chests, arms, cooling

their moist armpits—the scent of sweat
       and deodorant—and the music, their racing

hearts, their genitals hard and wet, aching
       for union, and the car flying, sightless,

into…the end that you know. Never mind
       the probable, prior details.

ANOTHER ETERNITY, A DEAD MAN'S LOVE POEM

after a CNN (Delhi) report, February 5, 2022

Let me start by saying, I'm sorry
      for all that you've had to endure:
they blamed you for my death,
      cut off your hair, smeared black paint
on that face of yours I so cherished.

A garland of soiled slippers
      around your beautiful neck
as they paraded you around
      after having you molested
by the neighborhood brutes, knowing

you had a son not yet three.
      Telling you that I didn't expect
my death to lead to this—
      though I truly didn't—
won't be enough. I'm sorry

from the bottom of my heart.
      But my heart—what is it worth now?
Just a few remaining flakes of ash
      doing the rounds in the burning
ghat, blown about for months

by the dry winter wind.
      If one of them could find its way
to you, land on your hair or cling
      to your skin for a moment
or two, it would tell you just how sorry

I really am. It would let you know
      (because this ash-flake would
be the closest any part of me
      would have ever been to you)
how the whole, the heart, of which

it's just a charred, miniscule part,
         skipped a beat every time
I caught sight of you. How it was like
         an unexpected gulp of water
quenching a parched throat

in midday heat, like the din
         of an ugly city suddenly sprouting
songs like the marigolds in my mother's
         terrace garden. The slightest glimpse
of you—your hair, a side of your face,

your bangled wrists, your lacquered
         toenails, as you sat in your father's
autorickshaw—made me feel like I'd won
         a lottery, the biggest prize
there was. And every time

your eyes met mine, a single moment
         was worth more than a lifetime.
An eternity, like an empty clothesline,
         stretched from your gaze to mine,
with nothing in between.

What is life compared to that?
         And I'd had many of those—
the last one when you said no
         for the last time, which you
were right to do—my heart was filled

to the brim, and so when I heard
         the voice telling me it was time
to go, I knew it was. I'd had as much
         as I was good for. What I didn't
know was that my leave-taking

would bring you such misery, so much
        shame and pain. I wish I knew
better. I wish I hadn't done what I did.
        I wish I could say this to you now,
standing at one end of another eternity.

BOXES

in memory of Agha Shahid Ali

There's a story in each one of them,

and a story behind everything
that's inside.

The one on her bed-
side table—hand-carved walnut
from Kashmir—

her mother had got as a wedding gift,
and *she* got it from her mother
when she became a woman.

(What better gift for a woman
from another?)

Years ago, it carried her

mother's lipsticks and kumkum box—
the scents of things past

and private still safe
in its dark, dry womb. There's a photo
of someone there—

a man lying on a hammock,
eyes squinted against the glare of a foreign sky—
the light fills her bedroom every night

when she takes it out of the box
to look at the face

and the body she learned so fleetingly—

and a letter from her father,
one of the last she ever received

before the bridge between them
had collapsed
into empty smiles.

There are secrets and silences
and lasting scents
of loss

in the box that her mother
gave her.

And she has other boxes.

I HOPE YOU LIKE THE CARD

The teardrops in this Man Ray photograph
look like drops of fresh rain, don't they?

That's how the message starts. It's a card
she made with a black-and-white

photograph she'd found in an old calendar—
blobs of silver paint around the picture

to mirror the teardrops on the woman's face.
I want you to know, she writes, how I'm feeling.

And I hope you like the card.

A duck takes flight
the pond wakes, leaping
then drops back to sleep

THE LAST TIME

She'd tuck the shirt in,
　　　tie the shoelaces,

comb the hair one last time,
　　　and after all was done,

she'd grab my left pinkie and give
　　　the tip a quick, gentle nip

and pretend to spit three times,
　　　and I'd be good to go

to school or wherever I was
　　　headed and be safe

from the evil eye or whatever
　　　she, my mother's older sister,

and mother to me, thought I needed
　　　protection from.

There was a day when she'd
　　　done it for the last time—

perhaps just that little nip
　　　on the finger, now reluctant

and already retreating—
　　　I wish I remembered

the look on her face as she
　　　let go of it, not knowing—

PREHISTORIC

I'm putting my son to bed.
He's almost seven, dinosaurs

are his new passion. I wish him
sweet dreams; he says to me

that he had a very nice dream
recently, in which he was

a triceratops, living a long happy life,
living alone, eating plants, and when

the catastrophe happened, he
and a few other dinosaurs

survived. Nothing happened
to us, he says.

I leave his room, wishing him
good night, his Jurassic picture book,

which he borrowed from school,
lying open on the night table,

a herd of prehistoric reptiles waiting
to dive into his dream.

INCENSE STICK

Staring at
      the burning
tip of an incense
      stick, my son
asks me, do you
      know where
the smell is?
      I shake my head.
He says, it's inside
      the smoke, which
is like a bubble—
      when the bubble
bursts, you get
      the smell.

LEGEND

Whether there was a king
named Minos or not

the alabaster throne
in which he (or some real-

life version of him) had sat
sits there

in what's left
of the palace of Knossos.

Outside the perimeter walls
of what's believed

to have been the labyrinth
where the Minotaur (or a real-

life version of it) roamed
two peacocks shrieked

in the afternoon heat
startling us.

TO BEGIN AGAIN

The right forefinger between the brows,
      then down to the middle
of the chest, the left shoulder, the right,
      and back up to the forehead—
twenty-five times in quick succession.

If I lost count, or if the finger didn't
      land on the right spots, I'd begin
again. Every single night, as the night
      watchman banged his stick
on the hollow-steel lamp posts to alert

the neighborhood to thieves and burglars,
      mosquitoes whining outside
the mosquito net. I couldn't fall asleep
      without the ritual done right.
Years later, for months in a row, my son,

aged eight, couldn't help touching things—
      walls, tabletops, his face—to feel assured
all was well. There was a method to it, too,
      a rhythm in which his hand moved
from surface to surface in a certain way,

like mine touching my forehead, chest, shoulders.
      If the rhythm broke, he'd
begin again. Outside his school,
      his classmate's grandfather walks
down straight lines in the cobbled square

as he waits for his grandson to come out—
      he picks a line, follows it till the end,
turns, and walks back up, eyes fixed
      on the ground. If anyone gets in the way,
he stops, then goes back. To begin again.

BLACK GRAPES

She craved black grapes. My uncle's wife,
childless and newly widowed. I told her
I'd buy some for her as soon as they were
on the market. The season had yet to start,

and I was going to be away for some time.
I'd never heard her ask for things before,
and she hadn't been doing well. *As many
grapes as you want*, I promised her.

She was gone by the time I was back.
Snakes & ladders and ludo, which she and I
used to play when I was a boy, remind me
of her now, and the taste of black grapes.

IN BLACK & WHITE

A man carrying a bull's head as if it were a jackfruit.
And a picture of two school-bound children in morning light—

smiling, they'd turned to face the camera in haste—
I remember worrying that I might not have got the shot right.

I wasn't quite ready, and had little experience taking
pictures. The man with the bull's head, on the other hand, might

not have even known he was being photographed, straining
as he was under the weight of the animal's head, sunlight

blinding his eyes. The other picture was of a few
willows along the banks of the river Thimpu Chhu, a bright,

gently curving road without traffic, and a building or two
covered by trees. Though no less banal, if memory serves me
    right,

these three stood out from all the photos we'd taken on that trip
more than three decades ago, using a Russian-made Zenit.

The prints and the negatives are all likely lost; in memory they
    keep
fading; so here, the most remembered details put down in black
    & white.

UMWELT

A conifer next to a broadleaf tree, in a corner
of the garden, lonely like a dog and a cat

separated from kin to be household pets.
The landlady said she'd have to have it cut

down. She meant the pine, standing where
the two cedar hedges meet. The neighbors had

written to her saying they were concerned
about their safety. They're right, she said,

nodding. See how the branches are hanging
over their passage? And what if it's toppled

by a storm? But what about the birds and
the squirrels? my children protested.

What will happen to them? Where will
they go? Why doesn't anyone think about

them? They were traumatized two summers
ago, seeing the landlady's gardeners pollard

the walnut tree with an electric saw. Ask them
to stop, my son cried, I cannot stand it

anymore. He hadn't seen the butchery
it had already endured. The trunk, sawed

off just above where it had started to
branch out in four sure directions, reduced

now to a wavering yelp of twigs. Perhaps
you can trim it a little? I meekly suggested.

Cutting it down won't be right; won't be good
for the *Umwelt*. She'd nodded; and later,

one of the neighbors who'd complained, told me
they didn't want the tree to be cut down either.

Trimming the branches would do. She mentioned
the squirrels and the birds, and I the Umwelt.

But someone was sent to measure the trunk.
One of these days, I'm afraid, they'll cut

the wretched tree down. And it won't be,
come to think of it, too remarkable an event

either; the felling of a single tree against
the incalculable continents of forests we've felled

for thousands of years. And for all that carnage,
take heart, there are more lifeforms in

fistfuls of forest soil than people on the planet.
Only, its needles won't sift the morning

sunlight onto the yard, and fifty-odd square meters
of the planet will miss its slow, gentle life.

And while the summer afternoons ablate
the garden's memory of it, the soil, now rife

with leftover moisture, will mourn its roots'
aborted camaraderie. As for the moon,

it will circle the earth a few times, rising daily
to look, weeping, for that evergreen crown,

and then, at some point, it'll give up and find
its perch on the walnut tree's deciduous bough.

And the birds and the squirrels, if still alive,
will surely have found their new homes by now.

A MURDER OF CROWS

Winter

early evening
a thick canopy of clouds

& a murder of crows
like fluttering flags
swarms of flies

bundles of arrows
gnarly necklaces

& long-handled spoons

turning
into wayward Ys

broken Ls
& many half-moons—
swaying

daubs of black
against the dark gray

coming together

in formation
then drifting apart

in loose tangles—
in sixes,
fours

& threes—
then a single

one

poised for a moment
against the vast dome

like an acrobat
on a balance beam
then swerving

in a wide arc
to let the wind

take it home

In the sunny yard
two squirrels and a magpie
they're surprised it's spring

WIND HORSES

1

Thirty years later, it's the fireworks' turn
to prevent sleep in Phuentsholing:
it's Diwali on both sides
of the Bhutan Gate.

An old woman in sunglasses,
lips stained red with betel juice,
poses, smiling, for a picture or two:
she's on her way to the prayer wheels.

2

In Paro, at a karaoke bar
named Ecstasy, people are happy
the way people are happy
in karaoke bars.

After midnight, when the stray dogs stop,
the rain picks up: a few loud men
and the rain-drum on tin roofs continue
till the small hours.

3

Tshering's parents are happy,
thinking their hard life is their karma.
He's training to become
a Dzongkha teacher.

And Dorji, a bodyguard
before, sells daggers in old age
at the farmers' market in Paro.
He's been to Darjeeling and America.

4

Green tents outside a house
in Thimpu, the night air lit with chants:
a young man has died.
The tents follow the last rites.

A trail vanishes into a forest
dense with silence, cicadas and birds.
In Tango Goemba, the monks wait
while a mountain creek flows homeward.

5

Outside Punakha Dzong, an elephant-
shaped hill; inside, the Buddha is flanked
by Guru Rinpoche and Zhabdrung Namgyal:
stories where no story is needed.

Two women sing Carnatic music
sitting under a jacaranda tree at the foot
of the dzong: their faces the brightness of air,
voices the lightness of light.

LINE DRAWN & REDRAWN

A man drumming his fingers on
  the back of an empty begging bowl

in Kolkata, all smiles, head bobbing
  to the beat. On Old Arbat Street

in Moscow, someone stood on a block
  of stone in front of the statute

of Bulat Okudzhava, local poet, long dead,
  reciting poetry, hands in the pockets

of his track pants, backpack on the ground—
  no one to listen to him. Later,

he sat alone listening to the busker,
  an older man singing opera songs

on the other side of the street. You remember,
  knowing how coarse-grained

memory is, shaped and colored by mood,
  light, how full of distortions.

In the few hours you had in Phuentsholing,
  you looked for the hotel where

you'd spent a night thirty years ago.
  In Paro, an old man walked clockwise

around a chorten, a badge with the image of
  the divine mad man pinned

to his chest, phallic symbols painted
  on house fronts to bring good luck.

At the farmers' market, Namgay said
      she hoped to see you again.

Pictures, a finite number of glimpses:
      life straddling memory and forgetting,

the way sunlight rode the fine line drawn
      and redrawn on your skin

by air and water as you stood waist-deep
      in the ocean one summer

in Normandy, your lower body numb
      with cold, a hot wind lashing your chest.

MARVELING

Dappled sunlight on the hills, red chili peppers
drying on tin roofs—the archers take aim.

A man walks into an empty bus stop and sits down
on the bench, a pigeon sitting on the roof—

one life a scaled version of another, the two
separated by the ways they throb and flit to the end.

Stray dogs, a dozen or so, around a traffic circle
with a concrete lotus painted pink, blue, and white—

some sleeping on the island's curb, some walking
around, as motorbikes, cars and buses pass them,

unperturbed. At Clock Tower Square, a man rests
his head on the shoulder of another.

The champion of naked manifest awareness riding
on the back of a flying tigress, curling flames

and blue-veined white clouds around him.
One morning years later, somewhere else, a fire-

crest will make death look easy when it will dart
into the glass window next to you and still instantly

on the patio. You'll marvel at how gracefully
its delicate eyelids will hide the violence of its last

surprise. Unaware of that now, your heart lifts
at the sight of a little girl darting out of a green door.

In the picture you take you'll find faces in the unlit
room through grimy window panes. Outside,

potted plants and prayer flags, and strings
of red chili peppers hanging on the wooden façade.

THE WORLD I SEE

The rolling, tinkling sound is gossamer-
thin—rising and falling, stopping and starting

like a child who's just learned how to walk.
Sitting at one end of the wide sunlit yard, I spot

the source: a rough-edged disk of aluminum
foil sent cartwheeling by the spring breeze—

each new gust lifting it up and carrying it further
away, making its ring wane a little thread

of pings at a time. What I see is how my mind
looks: *it* is the world I see. Looking closer,

I notice a foraging ant turn into an unmoving
spot on a brick-shaped cement tile as brightly

sunlit as the rest of the place: my son, whose
unintentional footstep caused the transformation,

the end of the movement, continues playing,
unawares. If he had noticed, he'd have paused,

taken a close look at the stillness and the texture
of the spot and pondered over its difference

from what it was moments ago. A gossamer-
thin pang of remorse might have shot through

his heart. *I didn't mean to…*, he'd have said
to me, hoping I'd believe him. Though there's

a world out there, where I can sit in the sun,
watch and hear a disk of aluminum foil being

blown about by the wind, witness the accidental
end of an insect's life, what I see is the fruit

of my mind, just as a dream is: a bit of what
it looks like now is a blemish on the cement tile,

containing a one-tenth-of-a-cubic-millimeter
ant brain, one-third the size of a grain of salt,

with 250,000 neurons mashed into exoskeleton,
eyes, antennae, mandibles, the tinkle erased

by the wind. In this world (& *there are more*
than 5000 worlds outside the solar system) it's now

time to go home: my son asks how much longer
he has to wait for his sister; he's hungry.

HERZOGSWEG

We're two to three meters apart, give or take, a barbed-
wire fence between us, a human and a cow,

one with an ear tag reading 44 254, both having paused
our respective acts: I my walk down Herzogsweg

and she her grazing, the pasture
rolling off the side of the road down to the shoelace-

shaped village of Seffent. I stand unmoving, held
in her slow, gentle gaze, her jaw working

in soundless mastication, her breath backlit by the winter
sunlight, an opulent udder straining to touch

the ground. We keep standing like that, looking
at each other, as moments pass. Two herons

and then another fly from left to right behind her,
and a man walks past me, also from left

to right. What is it like to be her, I think to myself,
standing there at this moment, intently observing

and being observed by another living being, one
that she's known all her life? What response

does my image (and what is *that* like? I wonder) trigger
in her head? What feeling-sensation-memory-

percept-thought, if any, beyond what
is already chosen, in some form, from the three-item

inventory of fight, flight or freeze? She bats her lids
and lowers her head, then raises it again. There's another

cow at some distance, seated, where the field slopes
down, and a few more grazing further behind. In the back-

ground, trees, farmland and the undulating hills,
and a few wisps of chimney smoke rising in the mist-

laced sunlight, and the turret-like towers of the hospital
jutting out like those of a medieval castle.

THE MYTH

a white rose lying face down
       on a cobblestone street,
              petals wet with rain:

the ceremony over,
       a young hawk alights
              on a bare branch swaying in the wind:

sights shrinking
       into thought:
              the now already then

*

an old man fumbles
       for his wallet at a flower shop,
              the florist wrapping roses in paper:

the stillness of a frozen pond
       lost in
              stillness   frozen   pond

the center and the periphery:
       the knower and the known:
              the myth of it all

BLINDFOLDED

Only the light and the shadow,
       and the way they hold my eyes,

not promising meaning, which isn't
       here anyway, but in memory:

the moment I, made as I am, start
       looking for it, I'm blindfolded

and sent off to dreams,
       as the light and the shadow wait.

THE PROLONGED NOW

The water's tepid wash
over my fingers, its swirl

and swash to the movement
of my hands, and the softening braille

of day-old starch growing in-
tangible, touch by touch, on the pot

I'm cleaning in the sink,
the warmth of the floor where my feet

are planted and the breath
at the tip of my nose—each a time-

telling thread woven in
the prolonged now that I am.

On this side of the door to sleep
a sky of shifting, shimmering
shapes of light

WHAT IS IT LIKE?

What is it like
To hold in mind
What you know
                holds the mind,
                the world & the you
                that *you* know
What is it like
To hold it
Like students do
                in their hands,
                in medical school,
                cradling
The doughy mass
Freshly freed
From its bony
                seat,
                its contours
                richly ridged
And furrowed,
Meeting light
For the first time,
                as they marvel
                at the universe
                within,
Wired by birth
And life,
The maps
                of the self
                & the world,
                the memories,
Feeling, fears,
Hopes & dreams,
The deep archives
                of color & likeness,
                the secret scenes,
                the vaults

Of passion—
All that &
More

        in the 90 or so
        billion neurons
        of this gray,
Flesh-soft mind-
Matter,
Now inert:

        you try to name
        what it's like
        for you
To hold in your attention
A similar one,
Your own,

        as it's busy
        keeping you alive—
        you feel its gravity
As you let it
Pool like water
In the basin

        of your mind,
        your mind wrapped
        snugly around it,
Pressing against
The doughy wall
For a better feel—

        and you still
        cannot tell what it's
        really like

SKILL

after Thomas Metzinger

As I watch these words come
      into being, letter by letter,
on the dull white (or is it gray-
      white? or a white tinged
with the lightest shade of blue?)
      of the laptop's screen,
there are shapes and colors
      at the edges of my sight I cannot
quite describe. Just as you can-
      not fully name the shapes
and colors of things filling
      the corners of your eyes
as you read these words now, whether
      on a page or on a screen
of some device. If you're hearing
      them being spoken, and if
your eyes are open, wherever they are
      focused, the edges of your vision
are taken up by ghostly bits
      of the world around you.
They're there, but barely.
      Every waking moment
of yours and mine is filled,
      like this, to the brim,
with facts we hardly recognize.
      If asked about them, we tell
stories—you and I—filling
      the blanks in our experience
of now with details ~~secretly~~
      borrowed from memory.
I know my world, or I think
      I do, as you know yours, or
so you think. So we talk
      about shapes and colors

and ineffable things as if
        they weren't so at all. And we do
a good job of it, too:
        they all believe our stories
as much as we do ourselves.
        Describing experience falsely
is a skill we learned in childhood.
        All of us are experts.

ME & NOT-ME

Consciousness is a metaphor-
        generated model of reality,

a *version* of the world around us:
        I lay in bed, unwell and weak,

reading Julian Jaynes. My wife
        thought I had a viral infection.

How are you feeling now? she'd ask
        at regular intervals. *What's*

your name? Later, hungry
        and parched, I sat at the table

with my two small children.
        "The characters of the Iliad do not

sit down and think out what to do.
        They have no conscious

minds…". *There are no metaphors*
        in their language, no

words for mental acts. My wife was
        calling my name over and over,

her urgent voice growing distant,
        sinking syllable by syllable

into silence. Then the lights went out.
        William James called

such an event an absolute psychic
        annihilation. My children wondered

why, instead of responding, I looked
        up at the ceiling, my eyes

rolling back into the head.
        The coming to was a slow fade-

in as in a movie. I found myself
        lying on the floor, part of the body

under the table, my wife talking
        on the phone—she was calling

an ambulance. The feeling was
        slightly vague, but there was no sense

of borderless infinity. I could tell
        the me from the not-me

as I lay on the floor, examined
        by the paramedics. I couldn't

get over Jaynes's claim that the pre-
        Homeric people didn't have conscious minds.

WHAT'S SILENCE IF IT'S NOT…

If you can get your mind to set foot
   in the body, coaxing it somehow

into the flesh-and-blood home
   it barely knows, you'll realize

that silence, if it's the absence of sound,
   is just an idea, or an impairment

displaced onto the world beyond
   the boundary of one's skin:

there's no silence
   inside, what with the relentless

bustle of breath and blood, the beating
   heart, the twitches and tingles,

the rumbles—the whole works.
   And if it's not inside, how can it

be out there? The *out-there* being
   the bigger scheme, which contains

the squashy wetware that contains you—
   this is what you'll see when

your mind's *in* there, and you'll wonder,
   what's silence if it's not

the inability to hear your own heart—
   the sound of the give-and-take

between the part that's yours
   and the whole that holds it?

HEARING

A car—tires on gravel, car doors.
      A door. Voices. A sparrow, a dove,
Crows, a magpie. Another sparrow.
      A duck or some other bird. An airplane.
Cars. Voices. Leaves. Two sparrows.
      A finch? A breeze. The breath. The heart
Beating in my ears. And cicadas in my head.

WHAT THE WITNESS KNOWS

An image turns up where

the dream fades—a fork
lying on a table—a dog barks,

a bird trills, the flutter
of its wings. It's early morning.

A word, a string of words,

a thought—*the vastness
before the moment shrinks*

into an event. The image
of a fork lying on a table.

What happens to them—

~~the thought, the image—~~
when they're seen closely?

The heart beats
to the moment's endless

iteration. The air cools

the skin. The thought—
being the sight, sound

*and smell before a witness
shows up on the scene.*

If the image (now a fork

with a pyramid of rice
before the O of an open

mouth) disappears, where
does it go? The thought—*then*

knowing what the witness knows—

if seen closely, where is it
seen closely *from*?

And who's doing the seeing?
Who's hearing the barking dog,

the trilling bird?

WATER & WAVE

Although there's no daylight between you and I,
like water and wave—the two being one, indivisible—
although, nested in you, I am what makes you what
you are, if it was possible for us to have a one-to-one,

I'd say, first of all, Yes, I *do* know more than you do,
(whatever *you* are independent of me) but less than
you may assume. I know that you've never wondered
what it may be like for me to be inside this airless,

lightless cavity, trying, for your sake and mine, to make
sense of the world outside, based on what the senses
tell me. It's never occurred to you how difficult that
task is: to make you go about your everyday life

and help you survive, I make *guesses* all the time
(constantly correcting the ones that are wrong) about
what it's really like out there. The room you woke up
in yesterday morning wasn't your own, though you

didn't know that for a moment, thanks to an error
on my part, like the dog standing on the edge
of the field was, in fact, a lost sheep, the man lurking
in the street corner the shadow of a tree, the blue

actually a green, or a shade of gray. Remember that
evening not too long ago when you almost stepped
on a snake while walking through the park and leapt
over it just in time? *It was a twisted branch of a dead*

tree! you'll say. It was, but it could very well have
been a snake too, which was why I'd made you leap
over it…just in case! Just as I make you either stop
in your tracks or run if I sense trouble in the air,

as I had that morning so many decades ago—what
was it? an improvised explosive, a homemade hand
grenade, that had landed with a thud close to you
as you stepped out of the house on your way

to school? No telling what would've happened
if it had gone off, as it was meant to, but you'd run
in the right direction, not knowing why, and the racing
heart had logged another page in our record. Without

you knowing, I make you do things all the time—
fleeting, ineffable acts that may lack the drama
of that lucky escape from harm but ensure our being
nevertheless. There's an un-told number of things

I've been doing relentlessly since the first moment
of our time in life to keep the body going, and I've
been doing as well as I can—keeping you alive
is in my interest: just as you're nothing without

me, without you I'm not anything either, and that's
the crux of the matter. And sustaining life—that of
yours and mine—being my responsibility, my role
depends on the hope that there will be a future—

a next moment, a day, a month, a year, and decades—
with you being alive in it, and it's up to me to plan,
for you, every single moment of that time ahead—
from your next move to pick up a glass of water

(so that the thirst is quenched in time, and the balance
of the elements is undisturbed for the sake of our
viability) to you doing each one of the countless
things you need to do to live your life. And my

guesses, on which every action of yours, no matter
what it is, is based, keep getting better. In fact, they're

so good, so precise—at least most of the time—they
make you feel as if *you* were in charge; you feel

proud of your abilities, not knowing that this world
that you think you're at the center of, is just an image
I've made for your convenience, putting you, an
image of you, in the middle to complete the illusion.

Although I'm the one who's done all that and is
running the show for you from moment to moment,
doing all the behind-the-scenes work, whether you're
awake or in a dream (although, strictly speaking,

you're dreaming even when you're awake), there's
something I don't know anything about, and that's
death—our death. This is what I meant when I said
I know less than you possibly assume. Because I

am what I am, and how I'm made and meant to
function, I cannot make sense of death—predicting
the end of life isn't a task I'm equipped for. What
that means, for you, is that you cannot imagine

what death is, as an experience. You cannot know
what it was like for your beloved uncle when his eyes,
looking up at your face, had suddenly stilled.
His death in your arms was an objective truth

you'd learned to accept—*So, this is it*, you'd
whispered to yourself. *He's gone.* And you know
that you will, too, as will everyone around you,
like all living beings. But it's beyond you (as it is

beyond me) to know what it will be *really* like;
how it'll feel when a breath will enter the body
and leave it for the last time. Because I cannot
foresee that and prepare for it, I go on making

predictions about life *after* the end of life, with
rebirth at times—continuation, you see, is all
I care for. So, I make up stories about life beyond
the finishing line here, and fill them with the most

cherished details of the one we know. And it works
for you, too, at least some of the time—you love
these fantasies about afterlife; you've spun tall
tales about them—not *you*, of course, I

am the one to be blamed for that: trying to hide
a shortcoming that cannot be overcome, I've over-
played my part—that's what I'd like to let you know.
If only I could: if only we weren't water and wave.

INTO LIGHT

Raindrops or hailstones (or crows/
        squirrels/cats) on the roof, or out-
side the door/window, voices, pleasant
        or harsh, music, whether your type
or not, rising from the floor below

or descending from the one above—
        if you can receive as a mirror
does, without effort, without bias,
        everything in front of it,
the sounds of these or other things

(a leaf blower, a hammer drill, an excavator,
        a garbage truck, a gong, even
an alarm bell)—receiving them, like
        a mirror, without letting
any of them, or any sign from your senses,

or whatever image, meaning, or mood
        your thoughts let fly
at your inner sky, interrupt the reflecting—
        letting them all appear, fully
formed, and dissipate as they please—

if you can do that, and *have* for a moment
        mirrored—not knowing,
doing nothing beyond only being
        awake—a moment
of a mirror's being, who can tell

if you haven't, for that instant, for all
        your flaws, been a bodhisattva?
A momentary buddha? And if that hasn't
        let something unfurl somewhere
into light?

NOTES

In "Cyclone," *Kanishkas* (plural of Kanishka) refers to the famous headless statue of the Kushan emperor Kanishka (c. 127-150 CE).

phiran ("Ganderbal," "It Wouldn't Be Alms"): a warm robe-like overgarment worn by women and men in Kashmir.

Attar ("Anjar 2001"): a fragrant oil.

pir ("Anjar 2001"): a Muslim spiritual guide.

City of Joy ("Lonely Planet"): a popular epithet of Calcutta that owes its origin to Dominique Lapierre's book *The City of Joy.*

doms ("Then it Rains"): a community of people (treated as "untouchables") who serve at Hindu funeral sites.

thakur ("Hibiscus"): a Hindu holy man.

chorten ("Line Drawn & Redrawn"): a Buddhist shrine.

In "Marveling," *The champion of naked manifest awareness* refers to Padmasambhava, also known as Guru Rinpoche.

In "The World I See," *(& there are more / than 5000 worlds outside the solar system)* refers to a NASA discovery reported in the CNN article "There are more than 5,000 worlds beyond our solar system, NASA confirms" published on March 22, 2022.

ACKNOWLEDGMENTS

I am grateful to the editors of the following publications, in which these poems, sometimes in earlier versions, first appeared:

Quarterly Literary Review Singapore: "Monsoon", "The Wall"

Poetry Salzburg Review: "The Foot from Bhuj, a Photograph"

Rise Up Review: "Not Our Colors, But Our Colors Now"

The New Verse News: "Leaving Irpin"

The Dalhousie Review: "Anjar, 2001"

Ink in Thirds: "Lonely Planet", "A Tall House Where the Pond Was"

Main Street Rag: "Wind Horses"

Rust & Moth: "Umwelt"

In Parentheses: "Water & Wave"

Arboreal Literary Magazine: "What the Witness Knows"

Poetry Breakfast: "Marveling"

Last Stanza Poetry Journal: "Amber"

The Passionfruit Review: "A Good Name", "It Wouldn't Be Alms"

Hamilton Stone Review: "Herzogsweg"

Journal of Expressive Writing: "Equilibrium"

Mantis: "The Spot"

Unbroken: "Hibiscus"

Detroit Lit Mag: "Line Drawn & Redrawn"

Neologism Poetry Journal: "Sitting on a Park Bench on a Snowy Evening"

ONE ART: "I Hope You Like the Card"

Dialogist: "The Closer to the Water the Better", "To Begin Again"

I am indebted to the late Agha Shahid Ali for his friendship, enthusiastic support, and in case of a few early poems, at least one of which is included in the book, helpful suggestions. Thank you, George Bilgere, for your close reading of these poems, and for considering me a fellow pilgrim. Thank you, Terry Hummer, for your insightful comments and suggestions about some of these poems. Thank you, Ned Balbo, for reading the manuscript. Kunal Basu and Steven Helmling, thank you both for your encouragement and unflagging support of my work through the years. Thanks to all at Redhawk Publications, especially Robert Canipe, Katherine Hickman, Patty Thompson, and Melanie Zimmermann. Finally, thank you, Natalia, Anastasia, and Yannick, for bearing with me when I wrote and revised poems instead of being with you. This book is for you.

ABOUT THE AUTHOR

EUGENE DATTA has worked as a newspaper journalist, a book reviewer, and an editor. His poetry and fiction have appeared widely both online and in print, with some of his work being anthologized, and translated into German, French, and Italian. A recipient of the Stiftung Laurenz-Haus fellowship, he has held residencies at Ledig House International Writers' Colony, and Fundación Valparaíso. Born and raised in India, he lives in Aachen, Germany. *Water & Wave* is his first collection of poetry.

www.ingramcontent.com/pod-product-compliance
Lightning Source LLC
Chambersburg PA
CBHW031143090426
42738CB00008B/1199